Home
&
The Surrounding Territory

by
Blythe Ayne

Books & Audio by Blythe Ayne, Ph.D.

Nonfiction:
Love Is The Answer
45 Ways To Excellent Life
Horn of Plenty — The Cornucopia of Your Life
Life Flows on the River of Love

How to Save Your Life Series:
Save Your Life With The Power Of pH Balance
Save Your Life With The Phenomenal Lemon
Save Your Life with Stupendous Spices

Fiction:
The Darling Undesirables Series:
The Heart of Leo - short story prequel
The Darling Undesirables
Moons Rising
The Inventor's Clone
Heart's Quest

Short Story Collections:
5 Minute Stories
Lovely Frights for Lonely Nights

Children's Illustrated Books:
The Rat Who Didn't Like Rats
The Rat Who Didn't Like Christmas

Poetry:
Home & the Surrounding Territory

CD:
The Power of pH Balance —
Dr. Blythe Ayne Interviews Steven Acuff

Home
&
The Surrounding Territory

by
Blythe Ayne

Home & The Surrounding Territory
Blythe Ayne, Ph.D.

Emerson & Tilman, Publishers
129 Pendleton Way #55
Washougal, WA 98671

All Rights Reserved

No part of this publication may be reproduced, distributed, or transmitted
in any form, or by any means, including photocopying, recording,
or other electronic or mechanical methods, without the prior
written permission of the author, except brief quotations
in critical reviews and other noncommercial
uses permitted by copyright law.

Book & cover design by Blythe Ayne
All Text, Photographs & Graphics
© 2013-2017 Blythe Ayne

Home & The Surrounding Territory

www.BlytheAyne.com

Library of Congress Control Number: 2010929832

Paperback ISBN: 978-0-9827835-0-4

1. POETRY/General
2. POETRY/Subjects & Themes/Places
3. POETRY/Subjects & Themes/Nature

BIC: FM
Second Edition

DEDICATION:
To all the people
who made me feel at home –
no matter where I was.

Home &
The Surrounding Territory

Table of Contents:

Two Homes....   1

Home

Spring
Crow Crop Circles	9
Nebraska	11
My Linden trees sing	14
My Friend	15
Bird music windsong	17
Making Bread	18
Spring	19
One More Time	20
Where	22

Summer
Summer-Spring Dreams	25
Letting Fish Go	26
Cottonwood leaves shine	27
Cloud Shadow	29
Small waves paddling	30
Peace....	31
Farm Girl	32
Sun Storm	34
Sunflower Seeds	35
Wide Missouri hums	36
What Trains Knew	39
Nebraska State Fair	41
Summer to Fall Equinox	42

Autumn
The Poppies	45

Trip	47
Solace	49
Softly like cat paws	50
Three Lindens	52
The Midget Goat	53
Good Luck Penny	55
Soggy leaves on trees	56
The Water A Gray Plaid	58
Autumn came last night	59
Far away chimes plead	60

Winter

Frozen winter lake	63
Anele	64
Tight As Bones	66
The Old Professor	67
You And I	70
Snow Cloak	73
Watercolor Landscape	74
Grandma Lehman	77
Monday Morning Laundromat	78
Transport	79
Haunting My Own House	81

The Surrounding Territory

Kimberly, British Columbia	85
Prism View	87
The Stairs In The Sky	88
Conveyor	90
One-Tribe	91
Eucalyptus Branches	94
Europe Hitch	95
It's a short dream to Calcutta	96
The 707	98

"She Created A Monster"	99
Driving Across Texas In An Ice Storm	100
Moose Jaw	102
Tying East To West	105
London To Mission Viejo	107
San Francisco	108
Legend	110
Cruise to Belize	111
Far away from home	114
Nova Scotia	116
If Wishes Were Camels	117
Thank You	119
About the Author	120

Poems in *Home & the Surrounding Territory* have previously appeared in:

Clover Collection
Colorado North Review
Greenfield Review
Hey Lady
MED&CA
New York Culture Review
Nite Visions
Nitty Gritty
Out of Sight
Pebble
Samisdat
Second Coming
Sunday Clothes
Talisman
The Fault
And others

Two Homes....

I've had the blessing, in my life, to have two places I call "home."

My first home, where I grew up, is the great plains prairie, close to Lincoln, Nebraska, in the very heart of the country, in the heart of the heartlands.

The home where I now live is ten acres of forest in the foothills of the Cascade Mountains in Washington state, near the lyrically beautiful city of Portland, Oregon.

The wonderful aspect of having two places to call "home" is... one has two homes! Two locations offer their gifts of comfort and familiarity. In two places I find people I know and who know me in a long, historical, and meaningful way. Two places give up their gifts of nooks and crannies and charms only known by long time residents.

The difficult part of having two homes is, when at one, the other tugs at the heart. I'm always a tiny bit homesick, wondering what the weather is like, what the people are doing, what I, myself, would be doing, if I were at the other home.

Home & the Surrounding Territory

Living where I do now, in the Great Northwest, double rainbows are to be seen every now and then. But a while back I went to a reunion at my "other" home, Nebraska, where we were enjoying an outdoor picnic during a hot, sultry summer day, on a beautiful lakeside patio.

Suddenly the wind whipped up, paper plates went flying like frisbees, lashing rain poured from gigantic gray thunder clouds overhead. Everyone dashed indoors, cozy and damp and vitalized by the drama of the instantly changing weather, the negative ions charging the air.

Within minutes, just as suddenly, the wind stopped, the rain stopped, the clouds turned into colorful pastel wisps. We ran back outside like school children, dancing in the refreshed, invigorating air.

Then, to the east appeared a gorgeous, rare for Nebraska, double rainbow. We mimed our joy under this miraculous phenomena, energized by the cool air. The two rainbows above Nebraska skies were, to me, a symbol of my two homes. My heart overflowed with gratitude and love for the vast and meaningful universe where I, one tiny sentient being, reveled in the beauty of it all.

Home

Much of the work in *Home & the Surrounding Territory* has previously appeared in various publications. The *Home* herein is about my first home, Nebraska. *The Surrounding Territory* is a small window into my wanderings around the world, appreciating the many places people call "home," while searching and searching for my other home. When I saw my other home, I knew it, having seen it in recurring dreams many times since I was a child.

If I had one wish come true regarding *Home & the Surrounding Territory* it would be that it reminds you of your home, even if your home is very different. I would wish that if your heart strings are plucked, the music rising fills you with gratitude for the blessings and delights in your every day life in the place you call home.

Childhood friend at reunion,
celebrating the rainbow light.

Home

Spring

Home

Crow Crop Circles

The crows cleave the unseen air
As deliberately as if it were wood,
Carpenters of the sky,
Messages carved, imprinted,
Make airborne crop circles....

Let them who have eyes see.

Home & the Surrounding Territory

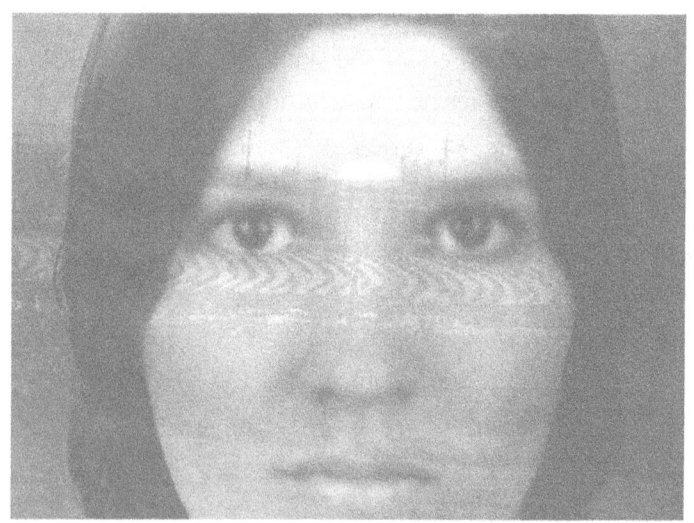

Home

Nebraska

I can tell about the railroad tracks
Glinting with abundant use from horizon to horizon
They have brought and taken promises
Shaken down and overflowing
Put bread on tables world-round
Brought new things from somewhere
Tools and tractors and fresh sawn boards.

I can tell about the fields
That flow and grow and kiss the earth with life
That make eyesight a wonder with such color
And justify humanity with farmers
Who build neat rows of rich soil
Turning it up to meet the sun, to glow black
And to welcome the seed back again. This is home.

I can tell about the miles of gravel roads
The likes of which postcards imagine in their dreams
Riding hills, roaming the prairie
Keeping company with golden rod
wild roses, sunflowers....

(continued)

Home & the Surrounding Territory

They meander in the moonlight
Flowing, ghost-white, static rivers
Not lost, just looking.

I can tell about the cows
Standing by barbed wire fence, watching the road
Waiting with patient wisdom for the moment
When they will jump the fence and flee to freedom.
They close their eyes, lifting their heavy heads
To the halcyon sun in pleasure
Imagining fields of gigantic, sweet flowers.

I can tell about the homesteads....
A big square house on the hill,
The barn and grain bin behind it,
Or a little bungalow among fir and oak
With the other buildings cozied up to it.
There are chickens talking gibberish in the yard
Mother watches a meadow lark singing on the fence.

And I can tell about the city
On the east end of the prairie
Where stands a golden dome
Believing in the sun, catching it, returning it
A wonder of the world
Not wondering, but knowing
This is the promised land.

Home

Home & the Surrounding Territory

My Linden trees sing
When the wind in them blows west
The song stops my heart.

Home

My Friend

You'll always be a farm boy
The gold of wheat and hay is
In your hair
And your blue sky eyes
Will follow narrow furrows
As long as sun shines
And rain makes mud.

Home & the Surrounding Territory

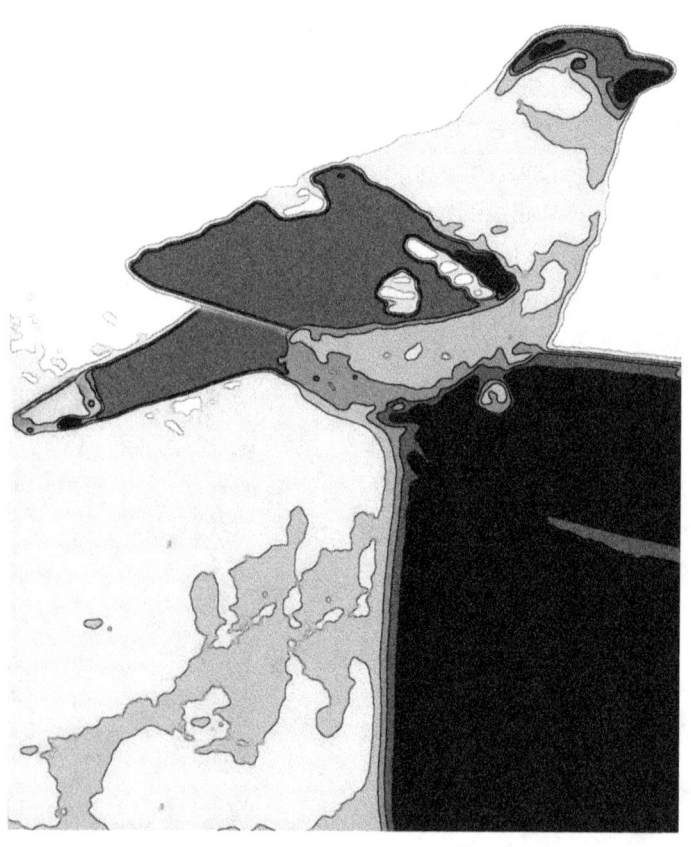

Home

Bird music windsong
In the woods find life it is
Time to take a friend.

Home & the Surrounding Territory

Making Bread

I want to make bread for you
I want to spend hot hours
Kneading & kneading
Doing what I know how to do
Let it rise
Then knead & knead again
And let it rise again
By the time you come in
Everything will be rich with
The sweet aroma
I'll spread melting butter
And we'll share a glass of fresh milk.

Home

Spring

I went out of the city today. Everywhere there is new green. Translucent baby green. It glows. Even under the heavy wet winter weary sky... this green.

At the lake I stood on the boat mooring, the waves high and white-capped. The water gray like weathered fence posts, but alive. The moor bobbed like a buoy. I could hear nothing but water slapping and slamming the moor, the rocks, itself... keeping fit.

I pretended to be voyaging the ocean on my moor raft, my body braced against the waves. The wind slashed my face with my hair, in it I smelled spring!

Home & the Surrounding Territory

One More Time

One more time I come to the paper
I want to write about this thunderstorm
How we've waited for it today, all day
All weekend the sky has been poised
Tonight it is too heavy
Heaving a primal sound the air
Changes to something I know
A clock face chiming, timing its life,
Mine. It will pass, it is passing now.

Home

Home & the Surrounding Territory

Where

Did those little poems go the ones about touching, a glance, sunlite on my blankets?

Summer

Home

Summer-Spring Dreams

Warm summer-spring
I'm lost in green –
Overwhelmed!
How, how do the years pile up
When each and every spring
The grass is the same green as when I was five?

Drive me to the lake
Take me away from this city where
Broken dreams gather. At the lake I watch you
On the other side fishing... you could be a
Little boy. Casting. Wondering.

Take me there quick! the cottonwoods
Are blowing a storm white blizzard.
I'm embraced by blue
Flowers in weeds, tadpoles, strange
Life in streams – something to take
Back to my dreams.

Home & the Surrounding Territory

Letting Fish Go

Last summer at the lake you went fishing,
Waiting patiently on the shore for hours,
"Just one," you muttered,
"Then we can leave."

And then
You caught just one... so small,
So small we knew it was too small.
"I heard you could stretch fish," you said.
I laughed
But you meant it.

Under my protest,
You laid the fish in the dust and stood
On its tail with your bare toes
Pulling steadily, carefully,
Your hand around its entire head.
I watched it stretch a good two inches.
You put it in your bucket of water.

When the game warden came
He said your fish was too small....
You threw it back.
It swam sideways, rapidly, away from us
As fast as it could swim.

Home

Cottonwood leaves shine
 Summer storms stir grass and ponds
 Then rest – leaves turn green.

Home & the Surrounding Territory

Home

Cloud Shadow

The cloud shadow glides overhead. My house envies it... its shadow lumbers around all day and does nothing original, goes nowhere it hasn't been. It sees that even the tree branch shadows get to skitter about on leashes.

Meanwhile, the most cumbersome cloud races my Jaguar down Interstate 80.

Home & the Surrounding Territory

Small waves paddling
Along the brown clay shore, wash
Away webbed duck prints.

Home

Peace....

Is a place to start often a very
Difficult place to start

It should grow like Spanish moss
Reaching from limb to limb not
Grasping desperately yet still encircling
Not rooted not uprooted
Just growing free.

Or like warm milk, gentle
soporific. Gently floating
On the night, the warm air warm like
Warm milk.

So peaceful.

Home & the Surrounding Territory

Farm Girl

Hair as long and auburn
and dense and straight as a
North American melting-pot farm girl
face made pretty by brown eyes if you like
brown eyes and hands that gathered eggs
made clothes baked pies hands that run
their fingers through blond hair callous
on the second finger right hand from pressing
very hard with pencils pens... for these hands
writing has always been something of a project.

Home

Home & the Surrounding Territory

Sun Storm

The storm is rolling in
rolling in on skates of
white egg white clouds
rolling clouds rolling
storm clouds the
white egg white clouds
carry the dark threatening blue
heavy rain and thunder and
lightning storm clouds
high and heavy clouds
lowering clouds storm
clouds.
The sun is shining.

Home

Sunflower Seeds

You!...
Yes you
Here
In this department store
A candy counter and
Sunflower seeds!
You leave me
And you leave me you
I remember
Sunflower
seeds.

Home & the Surrounding Territory

Wide Missouri hums
Sticks float, fish jump, sun shimmers
Mud banks hug water.

Home

Home & the Surrounding Territory

Home

What Trains Knew

Was it the tube of yellow paper
Daddy brought home?
Yellow rag,
Fluorescent pink along the edges
Oh, that was what got me
That pink!
I didn't know it meant the roll
Was almost gone and he
     could bring it home
Teletype paper
Telling what trains knew....
Was it the tube of yellow paper?
8 1/2" X infinity
     let me feel I could
Write and
     Write and
          Write....

Home & the Surrounding Territory

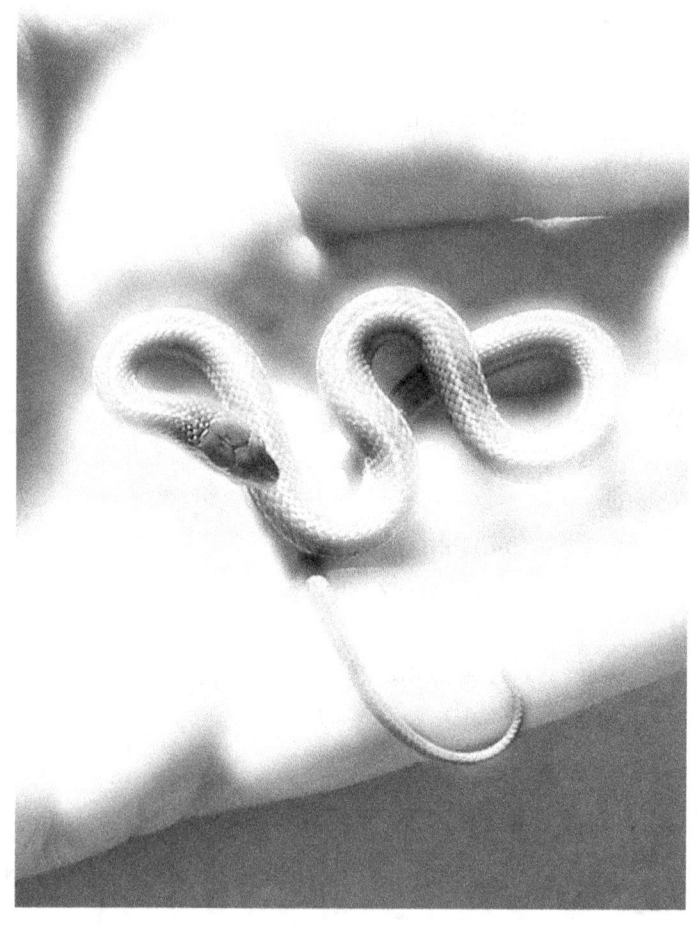

Home

Nebraska State Fair,
1912; snake constricts, breaks
bones of girl charmer.

Home & the Surrounding Territory

Summer to Fall Equinox

The full moon crisp
Clear sky makes
A good Nebraska hayrack ride night.
In town I drive my MGB among
Nearly silent streets
The mercury lights
Are one per block
Their light on the small white houses
Confuses with the fluorescent moon
Making sharp vignettes of leaf shadows
And cats on porch fronts.

Autumn

Home

The Poppies

Are through now....
Last week they reclined on lanky stems,
Orange crepe paper petals,
Now, there in the grass,
They lie like shrunken moths.

Home & the Surrounding Territory

Home

Trip

I discovered the back yard
A place I'd only glanced at through dusty windows.
I thought it dreary....
Mismatched fences and ordinary weeds.
But venturing out in boredom
I discover
The clouds come in to greet me,
The weeds caress my ankles,
The fences are not mismatched
But color-cued to guide me.
The astomatous bodies pinned on the clothesline
Wave
Good-by
Have a nice trip.

Home & the Surrounding Territory

Home

Solace

Autumn days
Wet puddles with slivery, silvery ice,
Limp leaves still vaguely green.

Some wistful sound....
A humid cricket, a squeaky bicycle,
A far-away siren.
Then – my front porch is cozy again.

Home & the Surrounding Territory

Softly like cat paws
Maltese patterned silent leaves
Pad across my yard.

Home

Home & the Surrounding Territory

Three Lindens

These are not leaves from any tree
Blown to any patch of ground. Big Lindens,
They shelter the house, you can see it from here.
                      I am like a Gypsy woman,
I am like a Gypsy woman, I sit rocking,
My hands fidget together, unconscious conjury.
                      Do I dream?
In the spring, seed pods spiral to the brown earth,
                      The grass won't grow there.
If I dream, I am sad – my dreams never bring me here.
When the morning is farther away I get lost in the night.
The Linden's leaves drift in the fall,
                      Pretending to be snow
Not pretending to show me time.
They were planted long before I was alive.
It's nice of you to listen,
I can tell by your expression you understand.

Home

The Midget Goat

The midget goat came up to the fence, lonely and not shy. His horns crossed over his head like two knives being sharpened against one another. One side of his belly was deformed and bulging. He was quiet and curious, his beard dripping wet. He crushed his body against the fence for me to scratch him. I did.

He smelled strange, a wild smell. He watched me closely with his augural horizontal pupils.

His companions were two small gray burros, their coats like dirty cat fur, clogs of burrs stuck on their stomachs, metronome tails chasing late October flies.

Home & the Surrounding Territory

Home

Good Luck Penny

Years ago I searched me round
and found your eyes a
rend in some deep place as if
light could be
left in a vacuum
Hermetically sealed.
                      That was Lincoln
at my feet
you found a penny for
my thoughts
you said
I said no, good
luck penny.
Found.

Home & the Surrounding Territory

Soggy leaves on trees
Hanging through the dusky day,
Fall in the long night.

Home

Home & the Surrounding Territory

The Water A Gray Plaid

There are slight ripples on Lake Conestoga, small and regular. The water itself, a dark green-gray, turns up on the small crests of the ripples. In between, the grays of clouds at two levels reflect. Three grays. Under there, as if the surface of the water is a separate thing from the water itself, under there fish live, and moss.

Where the plaid pat-pats to the shore it weaves in duckweed. I am on the moor. The end tied to shore is below water and below chlorophyll filled duckweed. The far end, where I'm sitting, is jutting up into the air. Two weeks ago this moor sat level and stable, and that day the water was not plaid.

The plaid water leaves me chilled to the bone.

Home

Autumn came last night
    Turned my house into a cake
    Frosting on windows.

Home & the Surrounding Territory

Far away chimes plead,
The few false summer days need
Warmth to sprout their seed.

Winter

Home

Frozen winter lake
Kerosene lamps, fishermen
Close around small holes.

Home & the Surrounding Territory

Anele

It is winter
I am relaxed on the orange couch
In the warm house, watching out
The panoramic wall-to-wall window.

Why do trees lose clothes when it is coldest?

The brick chimneys spout dragon breath
The dark birds perch on chimneys' edge
Facing in, silent around the brew.

Home

Home & the Surrounding Territory

Tight As Bones

She wears that great mass of night-watched hair
Pulled back, tense, unyielding.
Once, with a wide grin, it snuck loose.
Her hands like snake tongues
Whipped it back in place
Tight as bones.

Home

The Old Professor

Midwest man, bespectacled, bepaunched,
Be damned if he'll admit his age to himself,
Although he's more than willing to tell everyone else.
And who doesn't know? He retires this year.
He has plans, modest ones... no, not going to Europe
It's going to take a year
> to clean up that room at home he calls an office
> with its archival collections
> and letters he's owed for years to friends
> who may no longer be alive

People keep going out of this life... this life which
> used to seem so firm, so sure. Now it became
> a more peculiar stranger every year.

Well, he still had his wife and both sons, 'though
God knows they all seemed older than himself.

But it was always that girl....
Ten years younger!
The pain was not so much now that she had died,
But he couldn't rid his memory of the picture
Her daughter had shown him....
"The last before she died."

(continued)

Home & the Surrounding Territory

A smiling old woman. Who was she?
And traces of that girl were not on the daughter either.
It must have been a dream....
Such a girl had never been.

Ah! But now, to get everything straight,
To get everything in order before,
Before what? What a question!
Before the year is up of course
After that, then....

Home

Home & the Surrounding Territory

You And I

I was looking around
For you thought you
Might see me miss me
Remembering.

I saw on the way
Snowman in the yard
Someone's yard
Flower pots where
Eyes would be if he
Were not snow
But still man.

Back home again
A bee
Perfect whole yellow
Black dead by my door
Lying on snow
Wings spread

You and I
Oh.
I wish....

Home

Home & the Surrounding Territory

Home

Snow Cloak

Let us welcome in the
Great Ice Age
Let the snow creep
Over our planet
Uniting each to each
Houses to
paraphernalia in yards to
Alleys to buildings to
neighbors
to neighbors to
foreigners
cloaking ill will
Impatience and tight schedules
With the brotherhood-sisterhood of snow.

Home & the Surrounding Territory

Watercolor Landscape

Feathered snow
Linking houses to land to
Highway
Unanimous soul.

Home

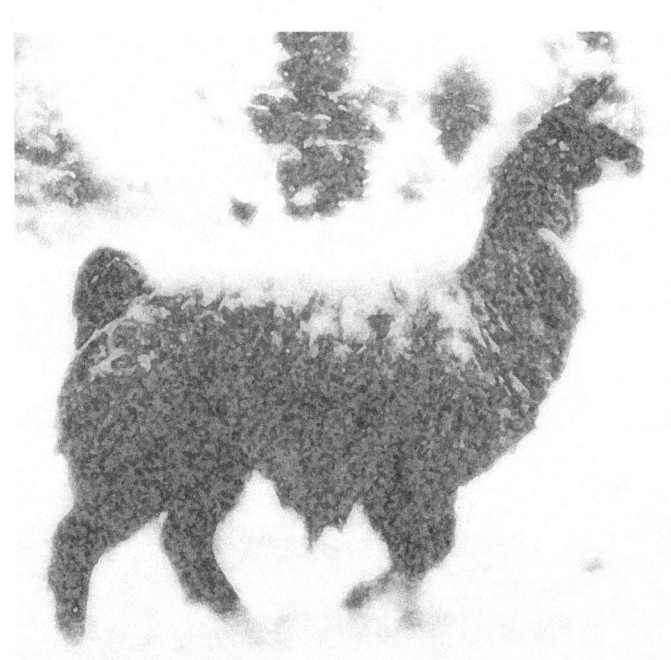

Home & the Surrounding Territory

*Alda Lutz Lehman
Wedding Day, March 2, 1887*

Home

Grandma Lehman

Grandma Lehman wore
Percale print ankle-length
Dresses and always gave me small change
I thought was so much money, and didn't
Know that so did she and orange
Slices sucking off the sugar feeling the
Ridges with my tongue almost too much
Orange flavor we both loved when I was
Seven and she was ninety. She'd had
A daughter with the
Most painfully small feet I
Have her button-top shoes
Who at twenty-one, walking
In a thunderstorm was struck by lightning.

Home & the Surrounding Territory

Monday Morning Laundromat

Limp skin on bones frail as a mouse skeleton
Bunching in resignation at the elbows
Piling up on finger joints. Years and years of use
all the places they've been to arrive here
Monday morning laundromat,
He with a cowlick
in white turning yellow hair,
She with a permanent contortion of the face;
surprised smile, raised eyebrows.
Forehead to forehead they
Sort through the whites the faded colors then
Shuffle together outside while the clothes tumble.
When they are dry, he folds his
She, hers.

Home

Transport

Night sounds
a creeping
sleepy train
snoring in the darkness
purring rhythm on
aimless tracks
carrying dreams of half
sleep to a distant morning.

Home & the Surrounding Territory

Home

Haunting My Own House

Don't look for me be-
hind doors
Or
Under the bed
That's where I would be
If I were here
        But hiding.
I am instead
Woven in the wallpaper
Stuck to the piano hammers
And burning burning
In the fireplace
I am
    lying in the floor-
    boards, running
     in the water
And coursing through the
Electricity in the lights.
Be calm when the
    strange winds blow
    The soft signing you
    think you hear is indeed
       me.

The Surrounding Territory

The Surrounding Territory

Kimberly, British Columbia

I fell in love with a post card
Fell in love with its mountains, and clouds
Taking off in the sky like
Freed mountains in rainbow colors
Tangling with the sun, the sun's rays
I fell in love with the flowers
Along the bottom border
Red, intense.
And love came to me on the lake
Placid dark gray
By the lake a little log house
With window boxes
More flowers
In the window my face
Smiling, my hand waving
Come see me, fall in love
With my post card.

Home & the Surrounding Territory

The Surrounding Territory

Prism View

When the day broke
We blended with the sky
We matched our talents to song birds
We felt ourselves rich like silver birch leaves
We studied every pine needle
Heavy with drops of midnight rain
Each drop a prism
Each holding its own view
More finite
And yet more infinite than our own
In each drop we were reflected
Minute and perfectly rendered
Again, again, and yet again.

In each rain drop
A holographic universe.

Home & the Surrounding Territory

The Stairs In The Sky

Look into the arcane eye
Of the timeless bird of prey
You'll see he dreams of the stairs in the sky
That he'll climb when he flies away.

Around and up, he imagines he'll fly
The earth far and small below
On the currents of air like stairs in the sky
Where the winds, like the rivers, flow.

How his heart longs for the day when he'll fly
While he sits on the pretty girl's arm –
But recalling the pain as he fell from the sky
He flutters and cries in alarm.

He suddenly knows he'll not again fly
Nor watch earth fall far below
Nor feel the currents' caress in the sky
Nor the winds, like the rivers, flow.

The Surrounding Territory

Home & the Surrounding Territory

Conveyor

Down the London tube
Clanking along the magic halls
Under the ancient halls
The city lives rhythmically far underground
Great escalators carry spectators past
The People's Art Gallery:
Men in underwear
Tights clad women
Movie monsters
Cigarettes
Candy.

Street level life in pictures
A perfect place to live.

The Surrounding Territory

One-Tribe

The strains of buzuki music
Thick as a palate of oils
Painting all colors of flesh tones
In music old as war, sweet as peace
That night!

We climbed to the attic room
Filling it with members of all-tribes
Gathering to prove there is but one tribe
That night!

Dance
The drums tell us,
Dance
Oh, we danced
That night!

The Holy Spirit of Music was among us
She wore a coat of many colors
She beat her feet to the rhythm of the drums
She moved her body to the song of the buzuki
She threaded herself among and through us
A strand of wondrous many-colored pearls
That night!

(continued)

Home & the Surrounding Territory

The Holy Spirit of Music entranced us
The members of all-tribes –
Man and Woman, East and West, Pale and Dark
And we knew we were most beautiful
Together
The Holy Spirit of Music bequeathed us holy insight
Keep the drums beating
Keep the buzuki strings vibrating
That night!

When we left the magic attic
The strand of many colored pearls was broken
But the memory of the holy thread
Runs through us still
The delegates from all-tribes
Are initiates into one-tribe
Our multicolored feet pass on the beat
Every night!

The Surrounding Territory

Home & the Surrounding Territory

Eucalyptus Branches

I don't know if it was pain or rain that woke me
But five-thirty in the morning found me watching
The night creep away from the San Bruno mountains
My back tense with pain
The birds beginning to make small sounds.

What I thought was rain was eucalyptus branches
Scraping against this foreign-feeling window
Its leaves clapping in myriads
And its seeds dropping in the sudden wind
To the ground like rain.

The Surrounding Territory

Europe Hitch

We were children then,
(We didn't know what we couldn't do)
Stowing away in the train engine,
Portable hiding place
Oh Lincoln, oh London,
Oh my blond Nordic husband,
We were inseparable tramps,
Huddling waifs,
Stinging snow, streaming rain,
Our one couple tent bravely orange
In the night
In the rain
In England, in France,
And, finally, in Rome,
Honeymoon hike,
We called it home.

Home & the Surrounding Territory

It's a short dream to
   Calcutta, the tracks divide
   Fantasy from sleep.

The Surrounding Territory

Home & the Surrounding Territory

The 707

Atlantic Ocean sunset sinking
prism, sinking 707 hovering settling on
New York, past the ships the water the other
side of the water to where the land is again.
I have been as a god, watching the tiny earth the
glaciers like splinters of ice, the little pinhead ships
While the sun and I race across the sky....
My beautiful Icarus body, my friend Ra,
Aloft on powerful wings,
Bigger than earth, equal to the sun.

The Surrounding Territory

"She Created A Monster"
(found poem — California state fair)

March 7th I waited impatiently for my first
4-H lamb to be born.
I was shocked to see that it had two faces!
Two faces on one head is called a Janus Monster.
It has four eyes, two mouths, two noses,
but it only has two ears and one throat.
The rest of its body was normal.
I talked to a vet,
and read books from university libraries.
I came up with two theories with how and why
this happened.
The theories are shown on other side panels.
Lucky for me, our ewe had twins
one normal male and
one two-faced female.

Home & the Surrounding Territory

Driving Across Texas in an Ice Storm

I leave Nebraska
In my little yellow pickup
Heading south
To escape winter.

Instead, I end up
Shoving it ahead of me
Inches of ice
Unfurling under the wheels
Mile upon mile
Across the Lone Star State.

The freak ice storm
Shocks
The stuffing out of the cactus.

As far as my eyes can reach
Stretches an alien landscape
Depth oddly flattened.

A diorama of a planet
Where cactus thrive in ice
Twisted into new shapes
Pulchritudinous ice cactus.

The Surrounding Territory

Home & the Surrounding Territory

Moose Jaw

In Moose Jaw, Saskatchewan
Early fall, a rain beginning,
I saw a black swan, alone,
Apart from the other swans,
(The white ones and the gray ones)
He didn't look at me once
I stared at him until it rained so hard
I couldn't see.

The Surrounding Territory

Home & the Surrounding Territory

The Surrounding Territory

Tying East To West

My father worked for the railroad
And I'd go stand on those rails
In the Nebraska heartland,
I'd see the rails meet the sun when it comes
And meet the sun when it goes
As a child I knew
They tied east to west.

And this is how I grew
Knowing I was to tie
East to West.

Home & the Surrounding Territory

The Surrounding Territory

London To Mission Viejo

Was I near you
Could you hear me
missing you across the continents....
Did you stop your work?
Did you look at your screen of data
And wonder why you thought of me?

It was night
The sky, overcast, close
The hot-house hot-pink
Glow of London-sky made me
lonely as I reached
for you I'm sure
I touched

Home & the Surrounding Territory

San Francisco

The houses climb up
Hills as steep as wishing, they
Hang onto the fog.

The Surrounding Territory

Home & the Surrounding Territory

Legend

There you are!
Magic and mystery
Out of an ancient story
A fantastic carpet
From a fog heavy sky
Where did you come from, Jinn?
When do I get my three wishes?

The Surrounding Territory

Cruise to Belize

Rocking like a little bird fetus
In the wooden egg of my room on the ship
I finally hatch on the shores of Belize.

The sky beautiful and blue, the air, humid
A shift in the green.
Orange, beige, yellow dominate.

I travel to a step pyramid with
My father and brother
A lifetime coming to this place.

Seeing them at the top of the pyramid
I gasp through the humid water-air
Gleaning molecules my lungs can use

Struggling up the pyramid, I think
I can get close to them here!
But I reach them just as they
Begin their descent to the pond below.

I have a picture of me sitting
By my brother at the pond
A rare, rare picture of the two of us together.

(continued)

Home & the Surrounding Territory

On our return to the ship
I lose my wallet buying a little step pyramid
Fear drips down my back—
No one allowed on ship without ID.

An angel watches—
A man comes up to me
Hands me my wallet
My ID, all my money
Disappears into the crowd.

What a miracle!
My brother agrees.

Back on ship I wander alone
Lost in a strange, foreign city as if
I've awakened in a dream and discover
The dream is real.

I encounter my uncle
We talk about... I don't know what
He wears a pensive, pervasive sadness.
I make him laugh.

It is the last time I see him
I'm saying good-by
Though I don't know it.

When we sail back
We each rock in our wooden egg room
And the sky is beautiful and blue.

The Surrounding Territory

Home & the Surrounding Territory

Far away from home
Knowing snow is leaving there
Imagine spring air!

The Surrounding Territory

Home & the Surrounding Territory

Nova Scotia

If only you were
As stunning as you were in
Halifax, Nova Scotia
The night we accidentally
Got along, the fight
Drained out
Leaving us
Pale and needing to
Walk in the snow.
My camera
Always watching for poetry
Pictured your long shadow
Across new snow,
Pictured your reflection
In the French shop window.
And when the dazzling snow
came down in
Weight-
            less
Chrysanthemums
Nestling in your hair
It was so beautiful
My camera broke into
tears.

The Surrounding Territory

If we had a camel
We could lope across the desert
We could arrange a tete-a-tete
On camel back.

If wishes were camels
Lovers would ride.

Thank You ....

for reading *45 Ways to Excellent Life*. Enter the following web address if you would like a gift of several posters with quotes from my book,
Life Flows on the River of Love:

http://eepurl.com/cKLPxn

*May All Things Bright & Beautiful
Fill Your Days
& Dreams of Joy
Fill Your Nights!*

About the Author

A Bit of Bio ....

I received my Doctorate from the University of California at Irvine in the School of Social Sciences, with a focus on psychology and ethnography, after which I moved to the Pacific Northwest, to write and to have a small private psychotherapy practice in a tiny town not much bigger than a village.

I worked with many amazing people, and witnessed astounding emotional, psychological, and spiritual, healing. It was a wonderful experience. But after twenty-plus years, it came time to return my focus to my writing, my true and original calling.

I live on ten acres of forest with a few domestic and numerous wild creatures. Along with creating an ever-growing inventory of books, my writing has appeared in hundreds of online and print publications.

Your support of my writing helps support ten acres of natural forest, and all its resident fauna. All the creatures and I thank you!

Questions, comments, observations, reviews? I'd love to hear from you!:

Blythe@BlytheAyne.com

www.BlytheAyne.com

www.ingramcontent.com/pod-product-compliance
Lightning Source LLC
Chambersburg PA
CBHW052026290426
44112CB00014B/2395